Yeah, But How Would She Look Beside the Go-Kart Trophy?

Yeah, But How Would She Look Beside the Go-Kart Trophy?

Nancy Jo Batman

Illustrated by
Skip Williamson

Chalice Press
St. Louis, MO

Library of Congress Cataloging-in-Publication Data

Batman, Nancy Jo.
Yeah, but how would she look beside the go-kart trophy? / by Nancy Jo Batman ; [illustrations by Skip Williamson].
ISBN 0-8272-4403-7
1. Batman, Nancy Jo—Views on conduct of life. 2. American wit and humor. 3. Illinois—Biography. 4. Women authors—Illinois—Biography. I. Title
CT275.B4886A3 1992 814'.54 92-19199

Printed in the United States of America

This book is dedicated to
Ray, Jay, Shannon, and Lindsay
who give me shelter from the storm.

And to Dr. Williamson.

Contents

SKIP WILLIAMSON

Mom's the Greatest (I Take After Dad)

My mother did not have a lot of rules for life, other than "Never go up the stairs empty handed," and "Turn the light on when you run the sweeper!" But through her example, I have gained deeper insight into such qualities as courage, perseverance, compassion, and love.

Courage: My sister and I took piano lessons from a very old and very white-haired lady who had a small parlor directly off her living room, where the pupil who had to go second would sit. The pupil-to-be would sit very, very quietly, not from good manners, but from fear—fear of being ripped to pieces by Mickey.

Mickey was a great, white Persian cat who made Lucifer in Cinderella look like he was on downers. If a fly buzzed around your face, it would have to buzz indefinitely because you knew if you moved a hand to swat it, you would never play the piano again. Mickey would eat your "melody" hand. Mickey would pounce on the cuckoo bird if it dared to cuckoo; he would pounce on the curtain if it dared sway with the breeze, but all of us kids knew that Mickey liked to especially pounce on piano pupils. And if you complained or screamed, Miss X would just stop and pat Mickey and listen to him purr, while we watched him Cheshirely smile.

One day my mother waited with me in the small, musky room filled with velvet, damask, yellow sheet music, and white cat hairs. I had repeatedly warned my mother not to move anything, but the erratic sound of "Londonderry Air" played by my older sister caused my mother's crossed leg to swing with a metronomic effect. I watched in horror as Mickey pounced on my mother's leg, shredding her nylons in an attempt to "get to the good parts." My mother shooed the cat away and firmly told Miss X that either the cat "goes" or her kids were going and reminded her that "Today's lessons are free, which should cover the cost of a new pair of hose."

The cat stayed; we stayed; but from then on, we got to sit in the living room with the piano and sunshine, and Mickey got the parlor. Through this experience, my mother taught me not to be afraid to swing my legs to a different tune.

Perserverance: During my growing-up days, I had a horse whose name was Sparky and whose home was the chicken pen behind our house until the neighbors got up a petition that you couldn't have horses in town. On the average of about once a week, I would glance out the school window and see Sparky running across the blacktop, hotly pursued by a perspiring, middle-aged woman wearing purple baggy shorts and a white blouse, and carrying a stick. Through the schoolyard, the neighbor's yards, occasional cemeteries, and farmers' fields my mother would run—chasing the horse who had once again gone over or under the fence. From these weekly excursions, my mother taught me to never give up the race...even when school kids are pointing and laughing.

Orderliness: In the days of my childhood-adolescent-teenage-and-early-adult rebellion years, I would make quite eloquent and moral justifications for a dirty room: "The world is not a clean place, Mother. It is a dirty place. I will be able to function 'out there' because I can go ahead with my life without straightening the pictures or dusting under my bed. I know how to work in spite of the dirt."

Now, I have to empty the garbage and clean my oven door before I type. When I was much younger, I had a great love for animals and would pick up stray dogs—bathing, feeding, and grooming them for the new homes I would find them. (They usually ended up living with Sparky in the chicken house.) I always had several cats, one of which had kittens quarterly in Mother's underwear drawer. Today, just like my mother, I am allergic to cats and, if given a choice between a clean carpet and a cute, fuzzy puppy, I would almost always opt for the former. I also like the following things which I didn't like until I became a mother: clean sheets, fluffy towels, socks on my feet during naps, naps, doilies and old lace, anything pink, the smell of roses and Pine-Sol, baths, new bars of soap, clean houses, and other people's pets.

Compassion: In the seventh grade I screamed when Larry Schwartz put a bug down my blouse. Because of the scream, he had to write: "I will not put a bug down Nancy's blouse ever again" five hundred times. He said he would "get me." I ran home from school and told my mother that we should probably move before supper. Just then, ten or so boys began circling our house on their bicycles—looking ever so similar to the crowds in Jerusalem on Good Friday (minus the bikes). My mother hid me, told the kids to go on home or she'd call their moms, and then gave me this advice: "Call Larry and offer to write the sentences for him." Through this incident I learned that when no moral issue is blatantly present, it sometimes makes sense to take the easy way out. (I also learned how to hold a pencil to avoid blisters.)

Idealism and Patience: Every Saturday night my mother would put my hair and my sister's hair into small curls with bobby pins. And every Sunday morning before Sunday school we would cry because we looked so funny. But come Saturday night, there she would sit—patiently pin-curling our hair. From those weekly sessions I learned that sometimes a "permanent solution" is better than a temporary one.

Sensitivity: Aside from the time she threw my doll named Dickie away because it stunk from the rotten food I fed it, my mother has always shown her sensitivity in obvious ways. She was the Significant Other at the graveside services for Petey, my pet chameleon who hung himself on her fern. She always gave the "thumbs up" sign to women going the wrong way on a one-way street in a generous display of camaraderie; and she named me Nancy instead of Patty like she almost did, and it has been much easier going through life as "Fancy Nancy" instead of "Fatty Patty." She didn't kill my dog who entertained eight boyfriends in the living room where she was to have a Missionary meeting that very night. And she didn't tell a date that I wasn't really a foreign exchange student from France and went ahead and fried chicken for our picnic.

Laughter: She loves reading page 563 in *The Science of Eugenics* (published in 1904) about the uses of capsicum or red pepper, which claims to be a remedy for "fat, lazy, unclean, clumsy, awkward, peevish, easily offended people with blue eyes and light hair." I don't really think it's very funny when she hands me the red pepper, but I like to hear her laugh.

My mother is a beautiful, brown-eyed, sensitive, caring, quick-to-blush, practically unlined, unselfish lady.

She passed most of those qualities on to my sister. I take after my dad, to whom she also hands the red pepper.

SKIP WILLIAMSON

Six Down, One to Go

It was Monday and it was raining and it was humid and I felt mean.

I was suffering from PEWSLAG. During the last several days, I had committed all of the Seven Deadly Sins except one, and there is a reason for that one omission which I will discuss later.

PEWSLAG is the handy way to remember the Seven Deadly Sins, which are: Pride, Envy, Wrath, Sloth, Lust, Avarice, and Gluttony. (I learned those when I attended a Catholic Bible study group in Bishop, a small country church near Dieterich, Illinois, where we used to live. Protestants don't mention PEWSLAG much. They also don't remember PALE GAS: Pride, Avarice, Lust, Envy, Gluttony, Anger and Sloth.)

I had been feeling full of Pride which is defined in my old, ragged dictionary as: "an overhigh opinion of oneself; exaggerated self-esteem, conceit." Pride is one of those sins that is hard for me to commit, as I usually am suffering from the opposite: "wormlike, fat; head full of ugly hair."

And everyone knows that Pride goeth before a fall. I don't know why that is, but I am assured that if ever I start thinking I am a little more than OK, I either get a job rejection, a nasty note, or the dog ignores me.

I had also been filled with Envy, which dictionary-wise means: "a feeling of discontent and ill will because of another's advantages, possessions, etc." It was the "etc." part that was making me full of discontent. I had written last month that I was feeling jealous of my friend, who was on a roll and was striking out on her own. It was even worse than I had imagined. She had found another man. Who among us middle-aged women wouldn't like to have that feeling of lightning bugs in the stomach—that feeling of being vernacularly "turned on" (the "L" word)? Although I am happily married and contented with my partner, I would like just once—even for an instant—to remember what it felt like to be sixteen and so full of Lust that I couldn't eat.

I had also been filled with Wrath, which means my eye ticked, my pulse raced, my lip trembled, and I said stupid things. Recent studies have indicated that anger is an addicting emotion; some of us *like* that rush of adrenaline. I don't know about that. I think I would rather drink caffeine.

On page 1374 of my dictionary is a picture of how the fourth sin looks. It's a sloth hanging upside down on a tree limb beside the words: "....laziness, slowness." Lazy and slow could be used to describe my actions lately. There is not one inch in the house that doesn't need Murphy's Oil Soap or at least a feather duster swished in its general direction. Spring cleaning comes at such a dumb time of the year. There is no way that a person would choose to be inside when she could be out mowing the grass, sowing radishes, or planting hollyhocks. I don't really *do* any of those things; I just *think* about doing them when I'm sunbathing. I have Tanorexia, which isn't one of the Seven Deadly Sins, but probably would have been listed if the Bible writers had anticipated our ozone situation.

Like I said before, the only sin I hadn't committed was the "L" one: Lust. And the only reason I hadn't committed that is because of the "S" word. I think it would be impossible to suffer from Lust *and* Sloth at the same time.

Avarice is defined as "too much desire to get and keep money; greed for riches." I don't know what "too much" means. I recently wrote some articles for the local newspaper about the Annual Home & Garden Show and interviewed about sixty exhibitors. One home builder told me that he is constructing houses that cost $750,000. "The master suite is 900 to 1,200 square feet and has a 12- by 14-foot closet and two bathrooms with Jacuzzis and color TVs." Those dimensions didn't mean much to me, but when my husband was proofreading my copy, he said: "This must be a mistake. That's the size of our whole downstairs!" (I checked, and the figures were accurate.) I think *that* should be the definition of Avarice—*wanting* a master suite that size—but my dictionary was written in 1951. (I wanted a pair of Army green sandals for $24.95. The sin comes in *wanting* "too much.")

The Seventh Deadly Sin is Gluttony. My dictionary doesn't mince words here. It says: "the habit or act of eating too much." In the past few days, I have polished off a package of Spam Breakfast Strips (which my husband says is not food, so maybe that doesn't count), five cooked brownies and three tablespoons of brownie batter, four pieces of fried chicken, a Mexican dinner with appetizers and chips, three other kinds of dessert, M&Ms—and why go on? You get the idea. Suffice it to say, the only food safe in the house during my gluttonous binge was Bingo's dog biscuits.

No wonder I found myself on the front porch on a rainy and humid Monday morning feeling mean. You can't commit six out of seven deadly sins in two days and expect to feel that "God's in His heaven; all's right with the world." Another thing Protestants don't do is confess our sins to someone behind a little curtained booth.

Pretend like you're behind the booth.

SKIP
WILLIAMSON

Gingerbread Houses and Impossible Dreams

"What's your next column going to be about?" Fred asked. (Fred Spannaus is my boss at Dove. He's the publisher of DoveTales and I'm the editor; that means he gets to say for sure where the commas go.)

"Gingerbread houses, I think. And one-upmanship and impossible dreams," I answered.

He stopped dipping his curly fries into the cheese sauce and said, "Huh?"

So I explained to him how I think certain people were put on this earth to make the rest of us stay humble and they do it on purpose and they're usually the kind of people who make great looking gingerbread houses.

He said "Huh?" again. (He's taking a course on How To Be A Better Listener, and it is really helping. He didn't used to say "Huh?")

I told him about a lady who used to send her small daughter to school with a lunch box containing the following: a hot dog with a string wrapped around it inside a thermos of tomato soup, a pre-mustarded bun, a Real Napkin, and an orange already peeled. At lunchtime, the girl would pull up the hot dog by the string, plop it on the bun, eat the hot dog, and then drink the soup and eat the orange sections.

"THIS SAME MOTHER ONCE SENT HER KID TO A SLUMBER PARTY WITH TOOTHPASTE ALREADY ON HER TOOTHBRUSH!" I railed.

He just looked at me the same way I used to look at my aunt Myrtle when she said she would never go outside again because of germs.

I think it's a subject men don't understand, like PMS and why it's impossible to enjoy a Christmas tree when the house is messy.

He just doesn't realize that there are Actual Women out there, who, when asked what they've been doing, will answer: "Well, I butchered a hog early this morning, then made waffles for the kids, which was kind of hard because the waffle iron is broken and I had to use the curling iron, then I tatted some doilies, cleaned the basement and all the closets, baked a couple of pies for the church bazaar—they love my homemade crust—ran seven miles, found the perfect color of lipstick, and let's see, I think there was something else before lunch....Oh yes, José styled my hair and I made a couple of quilts for the kids and a gingerbread house for a centerpiece for the dining room table. What'd you do?"

Well, I made the bed, looked for some earring backs, and read an article about a Decatur teacher who built an entire *village* out of gingerbread, trains included.

"What's this fixation about gingerbread houses?" Fred would have asked if he were done with his course and his mouth hadn't been full of curly fries and cheese sauce. He didn't, but I'll try to explain anyway.

I don't know when it started, this desire to make a perfect gingerbread house with white and pink icing dripping deliciously from the eaves; but I do know when the dream ended.

It ended the other day when I sat for two hours in a doctor's waiting room and didn't rip out a single recipe for gingerbread houses! I just nonchalantly turned the pages filled with Christmas cookies, meringue snowmen, fancy divinity (the kind you don't have to scrape off the waxed paper with a spatula) and gingerbread houses. I didn't once pretend like I was coughing so the noise would hide the sound of ripping pages.

Only a brief year ago, I hadn't been cured yet. I still struggled with the delusion that I could bake something someone would want the recipe for besides grits. I prepared "Goodie boxes" for my college kids. After a flour-covered day spent crying and baking and understanding the meaning of Infinity ("There will always be one more cookie needing icing"), I decided I would never again trust anything calling for cream of tartar. This year, I sent them ten bucks and told them to buy a pizza.

"What's the point of your column?" I'm sure Fred would have asked if it hadn't been time to get back to work.

I think I would have told him I don't have the foggiest idea, but I have the hunch I'm on to Something Big.

Besides, if God wanted me to be a good cook, she'd tell me where the rolling pin is.

SKIP WILLIAMSON

Oh, for an Empty Nest!

There is a disease I can't wait to get. My sister says it only lasts half a day—and she got *along* with her kids. It's the Empty Nest Syndrome. You can tell if you have it by the following eleven symptoms:

1. There is a dry towel in the bathroom.

2. There are no cans of Spaghettios or gnats around the house.

3. There is conditioner—yes, the kind of conditioner that you buy at the beauty shop; the kind they tell you will last six weeks if you never use more than an amount the size of a dime. And you won't even have to put it in an empty bottle

of generic conditioner and switch labels like I heard some mother did.

4. The car will have gas. The cupboard will have dishes. The music will be the old kind—like Connie Frances singing with herself.

5. The telephone will be for you and it won't ring very often.

6. "White Fang" won't be on the TV at 2 a.m. Neither will "Pump Up the Volume." There won't be videos lying under the couch that were put on your card and that you now owe $32 on.

7. You won't have to sneak out of the house. You can wear anything you want and no one will say, "You're not going out in *that*, are you?" Or, "Is that new?" You will be able to buy clothes and not feel guilty. (Maybe. This symptom isn't always present. Some say the Empty Nest Syndrome costs a lot of money.)

8. You won't have to switch the remote to channel 12 when your teenager walks in. You can watch a dirty movie if you want to.

9. You will feel better about yourself. You won't yell at anyone. You'll find you're really not as mean as you have been led to believe by certain family members. You'll discover that there's no one else out there in the world you will fight with as much as you will fight with your eighteen-year-old. There is something to that old saying, which no one has ever heard of: "Two women can't occupy the same kitchen." No problem there. It's not the kitchen that is the source of the discomfort and the itching. Kids don't eat *in* that much; they buy submarines and hamburgers and french fries and pizza until their graduation money runs out. No, it's not the kitchen that causes the friction. It's understanding completely that old saying and realizing the truth. Like that other old saying goes: "There are two things you can give your children: roots and wings." You'll discover that the Empty Nest Syndrome

comes at a good point in your life. Mothers have to grow wings too.

10. You and your mate will go out to restaurants at least four nights a week if you want to and you won't feel guilty. On the nights when you eat in, dinner will consist of burnt toast, frozen waffles, spoons of peanut butter from the jar, and perhaps an occasional bowl of icing.

11. The house will be quiet. No one will giggle. The dog won't wag his tail as much. There will be Scotch tape in the drawer—and scissors. There will be stamps and note paper and pens and pencils and hair dryers and shirts and glasses and spoons and ice. You may also notice you may wander into your kid's room—now that it's so nice and clean—and just sit on the bed and cry.

Every disease has its side effects.

NO HOPE
SKIP WILLIAMSON

Home Is Where, When You Go There, There Are Always Clean Towels

I spend my Sunday afternoons going through open houses. I used to think it was because I wanted a new house. Now, I think it's because I just like to see clean houses on Sunday afternoons.

The other day I went through one that had the usual house-type things: three bedrooms, garage door opener, 1.5 baths, clean shower curtains, and a young man sitting on the couch in the den holding a small dog.

"So, where do you work?" I asked after exchanging pleasantries.

"Ummm. I'm between jobs right now. I'm living with Dad for awhile," he answered and turned back to the football game.

In the sixties and early seventies, kids couldn't wait to get away from home. Their battle cry was "Hell no! We won't go!" (Most people thought it meant Vietnam, but everyone now knows it meant home.)

In the seventies, it was "Tune in, turn on, and drop out." (That meant they never had to do dishes at home again.)

The eighties never did get a good slogan. Not much rhymes with Yuppie.

Then along came the nineties and the kids holding dogs on the couches in the dens. Their most oft-repeated sentence is this one: "Home is where, when you go there, they have to take you in." (I don't know who said it, but a pox—and a couple of kids—on his couch.)

Not too long ago I wrote an article about the Empty Nest Syndrome and how worried I was about my husband and I learning to deal with the quiet and the order and the lack of stimulation provided by our graduating senior daughter.

The answer is, "We've dealt just fine, thank you." So fine, in fact, that I constantly feel guilty. We eat when and if we want, the house stays clean for a whole week, and our biggest decision on some evenings is whether to order pepperoni on our pizza. And we never have to tell each other to "Turn that down!"

One Saturday night, our recently departed high school senior came by to pick something up on her way to a party. We had a fire in the fireplace, Garrison Keillor on the radio, a pizza on its way, and only one small lamp on. She thought someone had died. "I never want to get old," she said sadly. We thought we were having a good time since our new goal in life is to be bored.

Just when we were getting used to our Empty Nest Syndrome, our middle child returned home from Athens, Georgia. She thought she was merely homesick and hated Georgia. ("They don't even have *fall* there. The leaves just die and fall off the trees!") But, after spending a few days back home, she decided to return to the Champaign/Urbana area.

My husband told her she was welcome to stay for about a week, but she couldn't come home to live. (That was not her intention, but he wanted to warn her that our Empty Nest had turned into a comfortable and fitting one.)

My daughter and I talked about all the kids who were going back home to live with their parents. "It's the recession," she said. "They can't afford to live on their own."

She told me about a friend of hers who went home to his parents when he was recovering from heroin addiction. (I think she tells us these things to make us think we don't have any problems.) After three weeks of staying in the basement, slinking into the kitchen only after the rest of the family had eaten, he was asked by his mother to take out the garbage. "I'd rather die first!" came his Ignatius-like cry. (Ignatius is the hero in my favorite book, *A Confederacy of Dunces* by John Kennedy Toole.)

He got better, and, I assume, so did his parents.

It's not easy having the kids back home—if only for a week. Take the matter of towels. They use four after their shower: one for their hair, one for their body, one to stand on, and one for their apartment.

Meals: They are all selective vegetarians. I was raised on corn-fed beef from my dad's store, Scotty's Super Market. Mealtimes are a pure hassle. They ask me things like, "Do you have any tofu hotdogs in the freezer?"

The Phone: Suffice it to say, they are not *careful* people. Our daughter once had a $300 phone bill and she hardly blinked. "That's because Barney called Yugoslavia," she explained.

Shampoo: For poor folks, our kids have developed expensive tastes in shampoo and conditioner and they use a lot of it.

Am I sounding like a Bad Parent here? Thought so. So just let me add this:

I love my kids. They are my favorite people in the whole world. And when they are all home for a *few* days at Christmas, I feel strangely strengthened and uniquely insulated. We laugh a lot and I thank God for such wonderfully eccentric and talented people in my life.

But this year, I just may get them a copy of Thomas Wolfe's novel, *You Can't Go Home Again*.

Just in case.

SKIP
WILLIAMSON

Yeah, But How Would She Look Beside the Go-Kart Trophy?

A friend of ours said something the other night that I can't get out of my mind. This was his comment: "I know four guys our age who are getting Trophy Wives."

He is in his forties.

I asked my friend Cindy if she had ever heard of the term *Trophy Wives*. She said, "Oh, yeah. Doonesbury did a whole thing on it. It's when the older guy divorces his wife and marries someone else, like someone twenty-five years old. And beautiful."

I honestly can tell you I had never heard of the term, and wish I never had.

A Trophy Wife is the thing that guy out in Boston was trying to get when he supposedly killed his. A Trophy Wife is the thing that guy in *Blind Faith* was getting. He, too, had to kill his wife. They both were also standing in line to collect millions of dollars.

This concept scares me. A sign appeared in Boston that read: "It's safe to come out. Just don't come out with your husband."

As far as I can see, both wives were beautiful. They probably belonged to that kind of health club where they play the music real loud. But they both had one fatal flaw: they were in their forties.

I have heard it said, or maybe I made it up, that a woman goes nuts when she's in her thirties, a man when he's in his forties. I figure if I made it through, by gum, *he* better make it through.

But I can see the attraction. Another acquaintance of mine was telling about his class reunion and said: "I was in the best shape of anyone there and had the prettiest and youngest wife." (It was his second.)

Another guy, named Chuck something, who used to live in Decatur and who is now a millionaire, was quoted in the local newspaper as saying something like, "I went to my class reunion like every guy dreams—a (some kind of fancy) car and a 25-year-old blonde."

I understand it. When I was in my thirties, I thought about 18-year-olds. But I certainly didn't think about killing anyone just to get the chance to make out again. Some of my friends didn't make it. They had affairs. Every one of them says she wishes she hadn't.

This is serious business. And where would you find a Trophy Wife? Are they on sale someplace? And if they're not totally perfect, are they considered Ribbons? And what if a guy hasn't quite made it up the corporate ladder but really thinks a younger wife would help him with the boss, but can't afford one? Will there be scholarships available?

So, since I kind of halfway understand it, I have thought of an idea. It wouldn't work in my case because I don't believe in it, but it's an alternative to killing and divorce. The husband gets to keep Wife #1, but he also gets to have Wife #2.

But there would be Rules. For instance, here are a few I jotted down during the last several days since I have heard the term *Trophy Wife*:

Wife #1 gets the VCR and the big toenail clippers.
Wife #2 gets the razor. The Epilady.

Wife #1 gets pictures of the kids.
Wife #2 gets the kids (if they're between the ages of twelve and seventeen).

Wife #1 gets to eat Polish sausage, Treet, real butter on English muffins and Little Debbie cakes whenever she wants.
Wife #2 gets to drink Opti-Fast.

Wife #1 gets to watch "Evening Shade," "Murphy Brown," and "Designing Women" on Monday nights.
Wife #2 gets to watch the ballgame.

Wife #1 gets to spend Saturday night eating buttered popcorn and doughnuts from the White Hen Pantry in her bathrobe on the couch watching *Nashville* for the seventeenth time.
Wife #2 gets to go to office parties and class reunions.

Wife #1 gets to dust Wife #2.
Wife #2 gets to dust the rest of the house.

Wife #1 gets to have husband back all to herself when he's in his seventies. It will be fun to hear about Wife #2, and Wife #3, and Wife #4… (they will get old someday too).
Wife #2 gets to be like Doris Day when she's forty and raise dogs.

SKIP
WILLIAMSON

Barbra Streisand's Jeans and Other Things That Amaze Me

I keep wondering if Barbra Streisand is happy.

Ever since I read in *Star* magazine that she will only wear a pair of jeans one time because she likes them stiff, and hence, took sixty pairs of new jeans with her on location—I just keep wondering if she's happy. (I also keep wondering if she's sane. Stiff jeans?)

But what if she has found the key to happiness and the rest of us are still floundering around thinking it lies somewhere in a package of Twinkies?

Sixty pairs of blue jeans. Let's assume they aren't the $19.95 back-to-school specials, but rather the $100 kind. That is $6,000. OK, let's give her a break and assume she got a discount because of quantity and they were in the $50 bracket. That's still $3,000.

I keep being amazed.

When Tammy Faye's dog had an air-conditioned home, I was amazed.

When Imelda had a zillion pairs of shoes, I was amazed.

When I hear a baseball player makes something around $35,000 per game, I'm amazed.

When I look at the property transfers/sales in the local paper, I'm amazed. (Houses costing more than $300,000? In Decatur?)

When one of my best friends tells me she wants a Mercedes that costs more than our house, I'm amazed.

Money just amazes me, and you will notice I haven't even mentioned $100 tennis shoes.

What is going on?

If I were convinced money could make us happier, I wouldn't be amazed. But it doesn't. It can't. No one *thing* can make us happy. Try eating one potato chip. We always want "just a little bit more" to make us truly happy.

I've "preached" on this subject before when I've talked about the lotto sign that read: "How much would make you happy?"

I think the question should be: *What* would make you happy?

One of my favorite books is *The Imitation of Christ* by St. Thomas a Kempis, which was first published around 1486. I try to read it each morning after I've read the morning paper, as a sort of neutralizing agent.

The most intriguing title of one of the chapters is found on page 114: "Of Four Things That Bring Peace into the Soul."

Blue jeans aren't mentioned. Neither are shoes, cars, houses, boats, or the perfect color of lipstick. Cinnamon rolls are also omitted.

So, what are the four things that bring peace into the soul?

1. "Study, my son, rather to fulfill another man's will than thine own."

But, wait a minute. This was written almost five hundred years ago, and things have changed. We have to take charge; we can't let others walk all over us. Besides, how can we tell what another man or woman is thinking? No, we have to look out for numero uno. Sounds good, Thomas, but very impractical. Let's look at number two:

2. "Choose always to have little worldly riches, rather than much."

Now, things are really getting crazy. That is almost communism, or at the least, unAmerican. We just have to keep remembering that this was written five hundred years ago and the Mercedes hadn't been invented.

3. "Seek always the lowest place, and desire to be under others rather than above."

I assume he was referring to sex.

4. "Covet always, and pray that the will of God be wholly done in thee."

Now, this one is a little easier to understand. Don't we all know people who have prayed for a new car—and gotten one? "It's God's will," we say when we land a huge contract or find the perfect five-bedroom with three-and-a-half baths on six acres.

I was talking to my daughter one time about these four things that make for happiness, and she said: "Yeah, but he was a *saint*, for Pete's sake."

It would be great if we could just ignore these ancient words by this misguided monk. It would be easy if sixty pairs of blue jeans were the key to happiness and St. Thomas would have expanded his list to include five things.

But, as you may have noticed, our way—the American way—doesn't seem to be working. People buy and buy; and still we don't smile. We spend and spend; and still we are restless and worried and choose Rolaids as our "drug of choice."

I wonder what would happen if we tried to live by these simple rules? What if we tried to find out what the *other* person needed instead of asserting our rights? What if we gave away some of what we have and didn't try to get more? What if we didn't try to always be first—even in the checkout line at the supermarket? And what if we truly let God's will be done in us?

Someone would probably point us in the direction of a good Assertiveness Training workshop.

Or maybe we would be dismissed as a *saint*, for Pete's sake.

SKIP
WILLIAMSON

Showbiz

As they say, Everything Works Out for the Best.

I used to whine because I didn't have a full-time career. Now I'm glad I don't. If I were gainfully employed and had to wear panty hose everyday, I wouldn't be able to pursue my musical career, which, modestly speaking, seems to be absolutely skyrocketing.

It started several weeks ago at the Country Star Lounge. On most nights, it's a regular bar (I suppose; I've never been there then), but on *Wednesday* nights, it's a dream come true for a person who has asked for Mr. Microphone for the past ten Christmases. It is "open mike" night. That means *anyone* can sing or play the guitar or bang the drums and people have to listen. (It's got another name, but I can't think of it.)

A guy by the name of Raoul, who wears a blue shirt with "Be There! Life's a Jungle!" on the back, owns the equipment and started the idea locally. He starts the evening off by singing a few original tunes and then asks, "Who's next?"

Folksingers, rock singers, and would-be singers stroll up to the live mike and the people in the audience clap.

I was sitting in the audience when one singer played a few chords to my favorite song in the whole world, which no one knows all the way through except me—and Neil Young—and this guy who was singing these haunting words: "There is a town in North Ontario..."

And that is when I launched my career as a "nightclub" singer—singing "Helpless" by Neil Young. I held the microphone, shut my eyes the way serious singers do, and sang along with the young man, whose name I didn't get.

That was just the beginning of my new career.

Since then, I pursued another facet of my musical/microphone abilities and entered a lip sync contest at a local celebration.

The contest started at 4:45 p.m., so about 1 p.m. I began practicing "Because I'm Blonde" by Julie Brown—a song that netted me first place in a talent show held at some friends' house about four years ago and that produced a second place prize at the Blue Mound Fall Festival three years ago.

As I practiced mouthing the words, I gathered my costume. I went with a two-piece, white lace number that I had purchased for $10 about four years ago. The outfit is actually pajamas, and my kids said if I ever wore it in public, they would never speak to me again. Since they weren't around, I decided to go for it.

When I arrived at the library stage where the competition was to take place, I asked the M.C. what the prize was. First prize was $200, second was $100, and third was $50. There were twelve acts. It cost $5 to enter. I had $10 to last me the whole evening. I quickly calculated the odds and decided they weren't bad, so I told him I wanted to enter. He asked me my name and I gave him my pen name and told him I was from Sullivan, a small town west of here.

I was number nine. The girl who was number eight told me they judge you on such things as How Well You Know the Words, Not Making Any Noise with Your Mouth, and Your Costume.

During the actual performance, I couldn't remember many of the words and made noises with my mouth, but I thought my costume was good.

The winner was finally announced and it wasn't me. It was a six-year-old girl who had been number ten. I didn't even place.

When I told my mother the next day what I had done, she said, "Weren't you embarrassed?...Were you the oldest person in the contest?" (I love moms. They know how to cut through all the junk and get right to the quick.)

I told her it didn't make any difference how old you were; there is always someone younger who wins things.

I reminded her of the Little Miss Sunbeam Bread Contest when I was six, which still hurts to talk about. My parents took me to a beauty shop for the first time and had my blond hair fixed in long curls. I wore a blue dress with a white collar and practiced smiling in front of the full-length bedroom mirror. I just knew I was going to win because I looked just like a stockier version of the picture on the bread wrapper.

The winner was a three-year-old and she received the $5 prize. Second place was a loaf of white Sunbeam bread, which I ate all by myself while sitting in the darkened PIX theater in Blue Mound watching a cowboy show that starred Tom Mix. My tears made the bread taste salty.

Ah, showbiz.

SKIP
WILLIAMSON

What *Is* a Veil of Clay, and How Do I Rend It?

We sang that hymn again Sunday. It's the one that always makes me feel like a crummy hypocrite every time I sing it. It's innocently called, "Spirit of God, Descend Upon My Heart."

It's the second stanza I have trouble with. The words are these:

> I ask no dream, no prophet ecstasies,
> No sudden rending of the veil of clay,
> No angel visitant, no opening skies;
> But take the dimness of my soul away.

The reason I feel like a hypocrite is because I want them all: I want dreams; I want prophet ecstasies; I want rending of the veil of clay (whatever that means); I want angels; and I want opening skies. And I sure as heck wish someone would take the dimness of my soul away.

In lieu of those, I will settle for burning bushes, finger-messages in the sand, or notes tied around rocks thrown through my bedroom window. I want answers. I want experiences. I want REVELATIONS.

In fact, I have often thought it would be tidy to have one of those big calendars you see in nursing homes that lists the day, the year and the weather. Only it would include a special section: "What I Want You to Do Today." It would be signed by God.

I think I suffer from Experience Idolatry. I seek for spiritual highs, even though that means suffering through the lows. I can't imagine a world without the *chance* of intense spiritual bliss.

I even tried to talk in tongues once. I sounded like a noisy gong or Vestal Goodman (Tammy Faye's friend who used to sit in that big easy chair and have a white lace handkerchief and call everyone "darlin"). It didn't work. And, here's something I've never told anyone: I am envious of those people who have had "near-death" experiences—where they go through a tunnel toward a white light, see their dead friends and family, and—at last—God.

My husband is the type who could have written that hymn. He believes a Christian should be steadfast, and cites examples of monks who lived their lives quietly and holy—baking bread, reading Scripture, getting up early in the morning, and dividing their days into such frames as Matins and Vespers. And then, he uses the one word that ends the argument: Clessie.

I've never known Clessie Dalluge when she wasn't old. She is a member of our home church in Blue Mound, Illinois. Clessie smiles, hugs, serves, and always has a kind word. "She is just a *good* person," he says, emphasizing the word *good*. She is a steadfast Christian, and I doubt that she has ever even wondered what a "veil of clay" is.

I can't disagree with him when he trots out Clessie during the argumentative process. But, since I don't feel like smiling all the time or hugging all the time, or serving all the time (and I have a hunch I'm just plain meaner than Clessie)—I want that instant kind of bliss: that second when God parts the veil and gives me glimpses of immortality and lets me know that everything will be all right.

I've had a few such experiences, but they can't be written about or explained. (I know. I tried.) They were mystical, and there are no words for mystery.

A friend said something the other day that I can't get out of mind: "I don't think I'm a Christian—but I want to be *holy*. And I don't know how."

I didn't know what to tell him. I think I said something Zennish like: "When the student is ready, the teacher will appear." (I say that a lot when I don't think I'm making much progress.)

I just know I'm getting tired of having a dim soul.

SKIP WILLIAMSON

A Woman Would Never Name Anything a Scud

The lady on the exercise tape told me to smile at that ceiling: "Somebody up there likes you—I know that they do."

Usually, that's when I can begin smiling. We get to lie down and we're almost through—only three more songs to go.

But that day, I just couldn't. It was the day after the war started.

I'm still trying to make sense of this whole mess, so bear in mind those words by Eugene Ionesco: "Why do people always expect authors to answer questions? I am an author because I want to ask questions. If I had all the answers, I'd be a politician."

Actually, I would be an Amish person. The local newspaper had a great third-page story about our local Amish population. Since they don't have radios and TVs, they didn't know about the war. They just fed the chickens, like they usually do, and went to bed.

Just think if we all did that right now. Everyone. Hussein. Bush. Mothers. Fathers. Soldiers. Children. Teenagers. Politicians. Or, just think if we had been living our lives that way every day for hundreds of years. War would not be thought of. Their lack of technology and connection with the Military Industrial Complex (I'm not sure what that is, but it scares me) would not have allowed them to participate in war. I swear, the Amish are the only ones making any sense.

I *know* I'm not making any sense. I'm tired and really grouchy. The days before the war, I participated in two peace demonstrations and went on a local TV show and said, in a perky voice: "I don't think we'll have war; I really don't. I think all these peace demonstrations will show Bush that the people don't want war." I said a lot of other things too, but they are probably just as stupid, so I won't repeat them.

I honestly did think we'd be able to stop the war. All we'd have to do is get out our old peace pins, try to remember what you wear to a demonstration, sing "Amazing Grace" and shout "No Blood for Oil!" in a loud and strident voice—and we wouldn't have war. George Bush would look out his window and say: "Gosh, I guess people don't want war. Look at all those people honking for peace and flashing the V-for-Victory sign. Get Hussein on the phone and let's see if we can talk about this—and get my jammies...."

So, I protested. I handed out leaflets and got tired of walking around the civic center after the first hour, and made up some excuse to leave. For the most part, people were nice: some honked, some waved, and one guy told us to go to Baghdad. Kind of a new play on that old saw: Love It or Leave It.

But then the war started. We heard about the bombs.

We knew who started it. George Bush. Oh, sure, he was provoked. But couldn't someone have suggested a killer game of Donkey Kong so they could work out their aggressions? Or that old custom of War Games that took place a long time ago? A day was set aside for men to hit each other with sticks. At night, they had a potluck or orgy or something. It was a day set aside for men to relieve their aggressive tendencies.

I don't mean to be critical of men. For the most part, I like men. I'm married to one. Half of my friends are men. But I bet you a trillion dollars if women were in charge—all over the world—we wouldn't have had a war.

For the first reason: women wouldn't know how to work B-52s and they would never name anything *Scud*.

Plus, I don't think women are that aggressive. We have other faults, but I can practically guarantee you that we would never have war—at least this kind of war. We might call each other bad names and spread rumors and cry—but we would never say: "OK, if you want that country, I'm going to get in a big airplane and figure out where in the hell Kuwait is and drop bombs on your city. If I kill a few thousand people or destroy a few old churches or mosques—well that's just too bad. I'll never say Uncle."

Or just imagine a woman not picking up a telephone at the last crucial hours. We would have talked. We would never have sent anyone to war. In fact, we wouldn't even have bombs. We don't buy things not on sale. Bombs are never on sale. This would be a good time to talk about the Military Industrial Complex, but I don't know anything about it. I just don't think we're in war because of oil. It has something more to do with money, but it's too hard to figure out.

But, I'm not sure that's even the reason we're having war. I truly believe we are having war because of men. This makes my husband mad and I don't mean him, or any of my friends—but there is something in men that makes them have to prove something to other men. Call it machismo. Call it aggression. Call it needing-not-to-say-Uncle first. Call it being a Man. But don't call it nice.

Transition: We have a new puppy and we are trying to show him who is the dominant one by holding him in funny positions four times a day. We are trying to get his natural aggressive tendency under control. At this point, I can't say who will win. He still hasn't hit the paper.

But, the point of that little digression is: We recognize the aggressive tendency, the territorial instinct, and we try to redirect it to a rawhide bone. We don't think the puppies are bad because they are born like this. They are just born like this. Both girl and boy puppies, I might add.

In the people world, I think we need to recognize these aggressive tendencies and institute War Games day. Have several a year. And if any women, like Margaret Thatcher or Jeane Kirkpatrick, want to play, let 'em.

But, what do we do in the meantime? We march—some of us carry American flags and wear yellow ribbons; some of us carry peace signs and yell things. Some of us just prefer to watch the whole thing on TV—like a real live video game. If we quit watching, we might miss seeing someone get blown up. Some of us point to targets on a map and talk about laser missiles. Some of us are over there fighting. Some of us are putting on gas masks every hour or so and shooing our children to a bunker and trying to explain why. And *one* of us is showing what he meant when he talked about "a thousand points of light."

But, we're all tired. Just when walls all over were tumblin' down, and we were feeling pretty good about Christmas, we turn on our TV sets and see war.

Just imagine if all of us just went home and fed our chickens.

SKIP WILLIAMSON

If God Had Wanted Me Thin, She Wouldn't Have Invented Little Debbie Cakes

My sister and I were huffing up the hill after a day of fishing and she said: "I'm at a new all-time high, weightwise."

"Me too," I said. "I blame it on God."

"Why God?"

"Because she invented those Little Debbie cakes," I answered.

Things like Little Debbie cakes and Twinkies don't just "happen." There is a Mystical Force behind "Big Otises" at Hucks' or Ding Dongs and the stuff inside Twinkies. The "Big Bang" theory might work with people (that we were created by accident), but we are talking Celestial when we open the wrapper of one of those oatmeal Little Debbie cakes.

I don't even know where or when Little Debbie cakes came along. Suddenly, one day in the supermarket, I looked in my cart and there they were. "Gee, I haven't baked anything for about a year; maybe those would make a good after-school snack."

They probably would have, but they made such a good mid-morning snack, lunch-time dessert, and soap opera companion, that there usually weren't any left for after-school snacks for the kids.

Having Little Debbie cakes in your home can make you very childish and churlish as exemplified by the following story: (We're not talking "Pack of wild dogs" yet, but it's a long way from Woodstock.)

The other night, my husband and I, both grown-ups, found two chocolate cupcakes that someone had overlooked in the bread drawer and that weren't green yet, and we hid the package. We hid it up high—behind the sack of rock-cleaning stuff on the refrigerator where no one looks or dusts.

Our eleven-year-old daughter came into the kitchen and started sifting through the bread drawer and asked, "Where's the cupcakes?" We said we didn't know. *Yes, we Christian grown-ups said we didn't know.*

Finally, we admitted we hid them but wouldn't tell her where and she said, "That's OK," and walked over to the desk in the dining room and pulled open the drawer and yanked out a carton of Pringles. "Ha, ha," she said, touchéingly.

It was at that point that we sort of knew it had gone too far. The next day, I went to town and bought so many groceries that I didn't know how to fill out the check and not one item was a Little Debbie or anything crunchy (except celery), or salty or sweet. We now have a refrigerator full of things I know I won't get up for and no one will steal. If I know there's "none of those Little Debbie things," I'll probably just forget the nightly excursions for oatmeal cakes and glasses of milk. I've yet to get out of bed to eat an apple. Or a carrot. Or anything green.

Some studies show that we experience the same "high" by eating chocolate as we do when we are first in love. But just as the reality of bad breath replaces breathlessness as the first love-high becomes a little more stabilized, the chocolate turns into cellulite and we are left with ten pounds of Little Debbie fallout at the end of summer.

I have learned from many past experiences that the worst thing I can do to my body is let it know it's going on a diet. "*A diet!*" it yelps, grabbing each fat cell and clinging tenaciously to it. "Quick, guys," my body commands, "you grab the thigh and I'll grab hold of that stuff hanging from her arms. If she thinks we are going to lie back and die of starvation without a fight, she has another thought coming!"

The only way to trick your body into losing weight is by filling it up with fruits, vegetables, some protein and lots of water and exercise, according to Dr. Martin Katahn, author of *Beyond Diet*. (Only he made it complicated enough to make it book-length.) Nowhere does he mention Little Debbie cakes.

Come to think of it, they aren't mentioned in the Bible either. Just things like manna. Maybe I've been laying a guilt trip on God and it's really only God's angels who are elbow-deep in chocolate and oatmeal and Twinkie filling. If so, I apologize. (I don't want to risk the chance of making him madder than he already seems.)

But, Little Debbie, if you're out there listening or reading this, remember these words by the late great Elvis Presley: "Are you lonesome tonight? Do you miss me tonight? Are you sorry we drifted apart?"

I'M SORRY, BUT WE CAN'T USE YOU ANY PLACE IN THE UNIVERSE!
ALSO... YOUR LIPSTICK STINKS!
SKIP WILLIAMSON

Rejection, Thy Name Is Nancy Jo

"What's wrong with your arm?" my friend asked, seeing the red splotches on my inside left wrist, which went almost clear to the elbow.

"I've been testing lipstick," I said.

That's all I had to say. She knew right away I was depressed. Whenever I get depressed or in a bad mood, I usually do one of three things: (1) dye my hair; (2) push the buttons on the Clarion computer which tell you what color of lipstick you should wear which always comes up a "2" meaning pink, and which I always ignore and buy orange which makes my kids say mean things about my lipstick; or (3) eat Little Debbie cakes.

This was one of those situations that called for all three.

I had been Job Hunting.

Like most women who either work part-time or Don't Work Outside the Home, I had been looking enviously at those career women who go to lunch in real restaurants; wear the kind of panty hose not found on the bottom shelf for 99 cents; have their own telephone extension, insurance benefits, retirement and pension plans and business cards; and have enough money to buy Skin Care Programs instead of what's on sale at Walgreens.

So, I finished up my bachelor's degree (after twenty-five years!), updated my resumé, read a book about job interviews, tried to decide what color my parachute was, and sallied forth in a new suit.

After six—count 'em: SIX—rejection letters, I headed to the Clarion computer, the hair care products aisle, and my friend Little Debbie. The number *six* does not include the number of stupid "blind ads" I responded to where you have to tell them everything about yourself, how much money you want, and provide a urine specimen and your firstborn—and they don't even have to tell you who's behind the box number. (Yeah. I'm grouchy. As my friend Cindy says: "Being rejected is like having permanent PMS.")

As a writer, I should be used to Rejection. My file drawer is stuffed with letters telling me what a wonderful writer I am, but how sorry they are their publication can't use my wonderful stuff, blah blah blah. My personal job rejection favorite is the one that includes the sentence: "With qualified applicants such as yourself, the decision was difficult to arrive *at*." (Italics mine. I wrote on the letter, "Never end a sentence with a preposition!" but didn't mail it back.)

I keep the rejection file for the same reason I used to keep dead ticks in a mason jar. You can re-read the rejection letters or stare at the jar of ticks and really have a reason to go to bed and cover your head and sing songs like "Nobody likes me, everybody hates me, I think I'll go eat worms." When you're void of sufficient self-confidence, it sometimes helps to *really* wallow, because then your luck can start changing sooner, or you can start laughing at yourself quicker. Conversely, the rejection letters and dead ticks come in handy to keep you humble if life starts looking too good.

And life had been starting to look too good.

Several months ago I thought about an experience I had with the Cosmos. At that time, I said that no matter what happened, "It will be all right." That was the message I had received while sitting in the middle of the woods on a night filled with a full moon and silence.

Now, here I am feeling not all right. I feel like I'm back at the Starting Line playing "Mother, may I?"

I think it boils down to the fact that my goal in life is to be head-hunted. I want someone to call *me* and say: "You're the only one in the world who can do this job. We'll pay you a bazillion dollars, and you get summers off, and you only have to work from ten to two if you want to, and you get a lunch break and we'll pay for it, and you get free dental care with all the laughing gas you want, and we think you're the best writer in the world. Plus, we love your lipstick."

Maybe I'll just get a new jar of ticks.

SKIP WILLIAMSON

Lint from the Suitcase of Life

"I'll put on what I'm going to put on in the morning."

The above quotation was in response to a question I had asked my husband as we were planning to go away for the weekend. I had simply asked, "What are you going to wear?"

That was his answer.

I always knew there was something *really* different between men and women. I think the key difference is packing.

I pack by first lying in bed about three or four days before the event that I need to pack for, making lists about what I will need to take with me. "Let's see, I'll need the hair dryer, the curling iron, makeup, a dress, shoes to go with that dress, another dress in case that one looks awful and I eat too much, hose, plus another pair in case I run those, earrings (enough to make a selection)....

My husband said *he would put on whatever he put on.*

That sounds so easy and makes so much sense. One of the persons I'm jealous of is Katharine Hepburn for her no-nonsense approach to life. She says when she goes to bed, she goes to sleep. "That's what you're there for," she said on a TV interview in her "I'm-so-sensible-and-you're-not-so-hot" voice.

I agree with Miss Hepburn and I would like nothing better in life than to go to sleep as soon as my head hits the pillow like she does. But the brain inside my head won't let me off that easily. No, that's the time my brain decides to act like a computer and starts giving me such pertinent data as:

- Your mother doesn't like your hair, but five other people said they did, unsolicited, so the question is: Whom do you believe?
- Waxahachie, Texas. (That's where *Places in the Heart* was filmed and I can't quit saying the word.)
- Your mother is usually right.
- Your head hurts a little; maybe you should take an aspirin before your husband gets to sleep.
- Are you going to pack your sweatsuit and shoes? If so, where?

It's almost not worth going away; it takes so long to pack and get there. And packing is the *fun* part. At the back of my mind is the little cartoon devil—the red one with the pitchfork—who lives inside a bubble and whispers stuff in my ear whenever things should be fun. Things like: "Psst. Don't forget what comes after packing, which, granted, could be fun if everything were clean and you knew who used the red suitcase last and where it is. After packing, as you well know, and I won't let you forget, comes *unpacking.*"

Unpacking the hair dryer. The curling iron. The gel. The hair spray. The shampoo. The conditioner. The hand lotion. The toothpaste. The brushes (including three for hair and two for teeth). The clothes. The shoes. The books. The magazines. The Christmas presents. The mousse in case the gel doesn't work. The vanilla extract. (I don't like real perfume. It always smells like real perfume. If I've got to smell something all day being around myself, I'd just as soon smell like an angel food cake) etc. *Ad nauseam.*

There is a game I play sometimes when I can't get to sleep entitled, "Walden Pond." I pretend that I'm Henry David Thoreau and am going to the woods to see how simply I can live. The object of the game is to see how much I can live without. It is a wonderful thing to try to imagine a simple and uncluttered life in the woods. No TV. No stereo (well, maybe a Walkman). No hair dryer or curling iron. No gel or mousse or hair spray.

That is usually where I get bogged down and have to resort to counting sheep because how could I miss "Guiding Light" for a year? What if I get real grouchy because my hair looks awful? Wouldn't it be better to take along the necessary hair products and forgo the dictionary?

My little cabin in the woods quickly becomes mentally filled with just as much junk as my real house and I decide to play the other game—the one I mentioned before.

Packing.

Now, if you'll excuse me, I have to finish doing that.

Aspirin
Non-aspirin
Raincoat
Other coat
Other coat
Walden Pond by Thoreau
Etc.

GIVE
FORMER CHEERLEADER
SKIP WILLIAMSON

Confessions of a Part-Time Cynic

Barbara Grizzuti Harrison, a writer I like, once said something like this: "I always hold my breath when the plane takes off. Who knows for sure that's not what keeps it up?" I hope that is close to what she said. Ever since I "organized" my files, I save everything, including what she said, and can find nothing. Anyway, I knew what she meant.

Who out there knows for certain that worrying and knocking on wood don't help keep the bad away?

After all, the bad usually happens when "you least expect it." Bad things "come out of the blue." "Just when everything is going great" and "just when he had it made." My theory is that if you're *always* ready, it won't happen.

George Bernard Shaw said it better: "I always expect the worst; that way I'm never disappointed."

Robert Duvall said almost the same thing in *Tender Mercies* while wondering why his daughter had gotten killed in a car accident. "I don't trust happiness. Never have. Never will."

My favorite literary hero, Ignatius J. Reilly in *A Confederacy of Dunces*, says: "I refuse to 'look up.' Optimism nauseates me. It is perverse..."

Now that we've heard it from the pessimists, let's be fair and hear a story about an optimist. A minister friend of mine, Dr. C. William Nichols, related this story during a sermon not long ago: "They say a positive thinker once fell out of the window on the 70th floor of the Sears Tower in Chicago. Every time he passed a floor on the way down, people heard him say, 'So far, so good.'"

There used to be a whole religion based on people who think like I do. They were called "cynics," after the Greek word *kynikos*, meaning *like a dog*. Cynics believed that nothing and no one on earth was worthy of praise and they snarled a lot. Like dogs.

I do some snarling, but I also do some smiling, so that doesn't qualify me to be a full-time cynic. Some days I think I'm more like the lady who used to live across from the grade school when I was a kid and kept all the foul balls .

If I ever get to be famous for a month (which is about as long as people get to be famous in this "What's Hot, What's Not" society of ours) and *People* magazine interviews me and asks me why I'm not an optimistic person, I'll tell them this story:

"I used to be very optimistic about life. I thought all you had to do was make lemonade out of lemons, turn your frown upside down, and let a smile be your umbrella. And then I went to college. One crisp fall morning, when I was walking to my 9 o'clock class, Margie—a cute, short, dimpled, tanned, black-haired cheerleader who was in the best sorority on campus—fell in step beside me and said, 'Hi, Jody.' (That was my college freshman name. I had changed it from 'Josie,' my high school senior name.) It was during 'rush' week, and I was thrilled that this sorority princess knew my name. I tried to act cool, and she asked if she could carry my books for me. We walked for a short time—she, enthusiastically asking me questions about my grades, how I liked school and her sorority. I just sort of babbled. Somehow, in the conversation, she asked me my last name. 'You mean you're not Jody...' (and she named another Jody's name who was also a freshman). I said, 'No, I'm Jody Scott.'

"She handed me my books and said, 'I've gotta run' and literally did so—assumably to try and catch up with the right Jody. I've never been very optimistic about life since."

People: My, you seem bitter about something that happened so long ago. Have you seen Margie since?

Me: Only in my dreams where Margie is now barely eking out a living as a fat lady in the circus and she wears her cheerleading skirt as a ruffle around her neck. Her dimples are infected, and her ever-present tan did what everyone tells us tans will do and has left her face a map-maker's dream. She has a beard where liver flukes make their home, and her hair has starlings in it, and funny things are growing under her chipped, brittle fingernails. And she keeps calling for Jody so she can say she was sorry and won't I please be in her sorority?

People: Aren't you exaggerating just a little? Surely you don't want *that* kind of revenge.

Me: Oh no? You should hear the future I have imagined for Jack Campbell, who went out for popcorn on a date and never came back.

People: And based on these two incidents, you claim to be a cynic?

Me: You know that saying about the glass being half-empty or half-full? Well, mine is polluted. You'll have to excuse me now...a foul ball just flew into my yard.

SKIP WILLIAMSON

I'd Probably Have Burnout if I Could Find the Stove

I don't know whether to pray in or out.

Does one pray *up*, as in looking up to the heavens? Or *down*, as in being humble? Or *in*, as in "the Kingdom of God is within you"?

While others are writing and talking about burnout, I don't even know which burner to use.

Recently, the kids were all home and I was at the point where I was about to stand a broom up in the corner and cut off the bristles, as described in a short story by Ann Beattie about how to make company leave.

Instead, I started praying: "Dear God, please help me be a Nice Mother today. Give me patience and serenity, even though they just drank the last Coke Classic and broke one of my grandma's "sherbet" glasses (otherwise known as "wine" glasses by non-Baptists). Help me to overlook the mess on the living room floor, which includes two persons lying on a mattress surrounded by congealed pizza, overdue videos, magazines, and my new glasses. They are my children and I love them, and they won't be here long, so help me to be the kind of mother who has smile crinkles around my eyes instead of frown furrows on my forehead. Lord, help me to forget all the things I think I need to do today and let me focus my energy on them...."

(I imagine God assigns me a lesser deity, like some lonely angel who likes to hear people talk. *I* even get sick of my prayers.)

Right in the middle of my discourse/prayer, I suddenly remembered the book that is changing my life when I remember to think about my life being changed. It is called *Awakening the Heroes Within* by Dr. Carol S. Pearson. It is subtitled "Twelve Archetypes to Help Us Find Ourselves and Transform Our World."

I had never thought in the archetypical mode before. She suggests we look inside ourselves for our answers because that is where the Spirit lives.

So I started talking to my Self in an affirming way, trying not to think what to fix for lunch if they stayed that long: "You are a good mother. You are a nice person. Most people like you. There is no need to be rude or unpleasant. You are in control of the way you act. You are calm, confident, and controlled. You are being transformed from a caterpillar to a butterfly. You are one with the cosmos, and as soon as your hair grows out, you will look OK...."

That didn't seem to help either, so I got out of bed and ran the sweeper to wake everyone up so they would go home.

It used to be so simple. As a child, my family would spend our summer vacations at Winona Lake, Indiana. My brother and sister and I would spend our mornings at "Bible School," our lunches eating Spam or tuna, our afternoons on the lake getting fungus infections in our ears, and our evenings sitting in the huge Billy Sunday Tabernacle.

Every summer, I would sit in the huge tabernacle, scanning the crowd for a cute boy's eye, sing along to the great old hymns, and listen to the various preachers who would yell and whisper—and sometimes cry.

The evangelist for the week would say: "While every head is bowed and every eye is closed, ask God to come into your heart. Do you hear that little voice in your heart that is telling you that you are a sinner? Why don't you—right now—while no one is looking—raise your hand if you feel you have sinned and you are feeling empty?"

My hand would go up.

"Now," the preacher would continue, "while the choir sings 'Just As I Am Without One Plea,' make your way down the nearest aisle and come and kneel at the front of the tent. Make your Confession of Faith today—while you still have time—remember, there might not *be* a tomorrow. You might die in your sleep tonight. Do you want to spend eternity in Hell or Heaven?"

By this time—every time—my knees would be shaking, my insides would be trembling, and I would find myself lurching from my bench to make the trek down the sawdust trail. I would stand crying before hundreds of people, trying to think up sins. I was "saved" for another summer.

It was years before I realized other families went to Pike's Peak for their summer vacation.

Now, I'm middle-aged and sophisticated. I don't even remember the last revival I went to, and when I sing "Just As I Am," I hardly ever think about stumbling down an aisle.

As a Level One Seeker (as defined in Dr. Pearson's book), I am "exploring, wandering, experimenting, studying, and trying new things."

The ultimate aim of the Seeker "is a fulfillment of the Self through transcendence—to be fully our own best Self and one with the cosmos."

Tall order. Especially when I'm still trying to find the stove.

SKIP WILLIAMSON

From Things That *Don't* Go Bump in the Night, Good Lord, Deliver Me

Certain magazines are always asking famous writers to tell why they live where they live.

I think the reason I've never been asked is *because* I live where I live. There are just too many things "bugging me."

We live in the woods.

"So did Thoreau," you might say, "and look at the great stuff he wrote."

"Yeah," I'd probably reply, "but I bet he didn't have a snake in his Barbie Doll house."

We did. My son found it one day when he was walking by the room where my daughter keeps her "haven't-had-a-date-in-three-years-Barbie" and her lonely kingdom. We managed to tell Ray (my husband) about the snake by using guttural grunts and pointing. We gasped that it was about 3 feet long and had rattles. (Come to find out, it was an 18-inch garter snake, but one never knows about things that *don't* go "bump" in the night.)

"Big deal," you say. "Ernest Hemingway had to fight bulls, and people asked him why he lived where he lived when he lived."

Yeah, but Hemingway at least knew in which general direction the bull might be coming from. Snakes never warn you ahead of time. They don't paw the ground loudly or snort or moo. They just lie quietly in wait—trying to pretend they're rubber until they're sure everyone concerned has had a heart attack, and then curl up in Ken's Corvette.

But snakes aren't the only critters who live in the woods and have made our house their little "place to get away to when every mile seems two." One night, my husband went into the bathroom wearing a purple mitten. I try not to ask too many questions during the first week of summer camp, as camp managers are known to do strange things sometimes, but the mitten was a new twist in "high kink." So I asked.

He said, "I need to get a critter out of there."

"What kind of critter?"

"A mouse."

"Where?!"

"Don't ask," he advised.

I asked.

"In the toilet bowl," he answered.

"And what is a mouse doing in the toilet bowl?" I asked, feigning non-hysteria.

"The mousey-paddle," was his cute reply. He rescued the mouse, scooping it up with his purple mitten and throwing him out the window. The next day, I found its nest in the bottom drawer of the oven, which it had redone in a lovely, paisley print.

Did I just hear someone mention Herman Melville and *Moby Dick*? My response to that comment is that the ocean isn't nearly as personal as one's toilet.

And speaking of toilets reminds me of toilet paper and the lizard I found in a new roll last summer. Try being casually seated, calmly reading the label in your underwear because you forgot to take a magazine with you, and having a lizard fall in your lap—then see if you can remember your ABCs—let alone think up a novel that will be so famous that magazine editors will ask you why you live where you live. We also found a dead lizard behind the cushion on the couch.

Or how about this *thing* I found on the floor one day? It was light green and about three-quarters of an inch in diameter. I twirled it around in my hand, feeling it with my fingers, and then asked, "Anyone lose the set out of his ring?" Then, I felt something moving and noticed the ring-set had very tiny, but very real legs. It was a TICK: an engorged, pregnant, evil tick—a tick about ready to hatch thousands of baby ticks somewhere in my carpet. Shoot. Stephen King had it made. All he had to write about were little kids spelling "MURDER" backwards on walls, and girls getting laughed at at proms and making the whole town burn up.

Another reason I'm not a famous writer is the matter of the "things" that appear silently and magically in the corner of our bathroom, right beside the shower—usually overnight. TOADSTOOLS. Try writing great poetry after that.

Besides the moving things, I also itch almost everywhere, and everyone knows it's impossible to write a sonnet when you have to stop and scratch ringworm.

I have also been bitten by a poisonous brown recluse spider, which I can't talk about. OK. I'll talk a little about them, but I won't dignify their lifestyle by donating an entire *book* to them. They are more disgusting than ticks. They hide anywhere and bug spray won't kill them unless it's a direct hit, and then they just laugh. They *do* bug spray. They walk on their "tippy-toes"—the little sissy-creeps—and hardly any of the poison gets on their feet, so they don't lick it off and die like any respectable spider does. They can go for months without eating. And their bites leave you itching for a year. They especially like big toes.

And I haven't even mentioned those triangular-winged flies that bite or sweat bees or wasps.

One day last week, I awoke and found a note Scotch-taped to the bathroom door. It read: "There's a frog in the bathtub."

There was. And it wasn't plastic.

Try explaining that to Oprah.

SKIP
WILLIAMSON

Aunt Rea and Ronald Reagan

I have an Aunt Rea (who really isn't an aunt, but she loaned my dad $500 to buy his first business, so we always called her Aunt) who was a county health nurse all of her life and now lives in a nursing home south of here.

I don't visit her much. To be truthful, I think I make her nervous. She keeps trying to remember who I am. But once I visited her with two of my kids. She spent the whole visiting time taking our medical history and writing things down in a little black book—taking special care to note the dates of birth.

Before leaving, I asked the nurse at the desk if she cared if I bought her a stethoscope. She was upset because she couldn't find hers. The nurse thought that wouldn't be such a good idea: "We like to keep our patients in a state of reality and she needs to remember she is no longer a nurse."

Why?

She hasn't been in a state of reality for the past ten years, but the one she's now living in doesn't seem too bad most of the time. She talks a lot about her mother and father and quilts and horse rides. She was thorough when it came to questions about TB and polio—her two most dreaded diseases. She had polio when she was ten and could never sleep on a pillow again. She was the one who helped scare my mom so much about polio that I didn't get to go to the state fair when I was in 4-H and won "second runner-up" in demonstrations with my "How to Pack a Picnic Basket" speech. (If you got polio, you had to live in an iron lung, which was sometimes demonstrated at the county fair.)

I don't think my Aunt Rea has any idea where she is now. I don't think she remembers how to cure sinuses any more. She mostly just sits. My dad still goes to visit her, and used to sing hymns with her like "Silent Night." She wouldn't talk, but she would sing. And maybe check his pulse.

I think the staff would have been better off letting her think she was a nurse and scheduling regular hours for her and "patients" who would be sick of TV and in need of a diversion. They could spend five minutes talking with my Aunt Rea—the Registered Nurse—by appointment only—about their problems, and maybe get their temperatures taken and be listened to.

This article is not about my Aunt Rea, however. It is about Ronald Reagan. I don't want to be mean because it's spring and I would like to feel good, but I think the man is at the stage where he should be a "pretend" president. We could give him a globe that glows in the dark and a wall map, and those black snake-things you used to light on the Fourth of July that messed up the sidewalk but were harmless, and a cherry bomb for emergencies in case he gets the urge to hear a loud boom, and some tin soldiers. We could also give him some of those balsa-wood airplanes that used to break the first time you threw them, and maybe a submarine for the bathtub.

We would let him live in the White House so he wouldn't feel away from home—or maybe he could live at his ranch. He says the ranch keeps him from worrying about "world problems," so maybe we should make it the White House. I'm of the opinion that a president is *paid* to worry.

We'll tell him where Nicaragua is and say "ENEMY!" and let him figure something out. But he can only use one cherry bomb, and he must be aware that not only will all the Communists go away, but so will we if he uses it.

We will let Nancy Reagan order china and talk about dope with Mr. T. We might let his grandchildren come to visit on Sundays, if they don't upset him. We can let him say "Make my day!" to the doctors and kitchen staff or even a Communist. (We'll paint some of the soldiers red so he can tell who's who.)

We'll let him watch that "Win one for the Gipper" movie as many times as he wants to or has time for. But under no circumstances should we let him "out."

The time I took my Aunt Rea "out," she just cried and cried because she had to get home to make supper for her father and asked why I was taking her back to that place (the nursing home).

What would really be great is if my Aunt Rea and Ronald Reagan could get together in the same home. He can have war and she can bandage him up.

(I wrote this during the previous administration. If you'd rather substitute "George Bush"—or whoever happens to be president by now—and "Iraq" for "Nicaragua" and "Saddam Hussein" for "Communists," feel free.)

SKIP WILLIAMSON

Reader's Block

I woke up this morning with nothing that needed to be done. Nothing was written on my calendar; I had no lists of Things To Do. The latest newsletter had been edited and taken to the printers and no deadline loomed over my immediate horizon.

The sky was gray and the paper said there was an 80 percent chance of rain, and a cool breeze was coming in through the bedroom window.

"I think I'll just stay in bed and read all day," I told my husband as he was leaving for work. He said that sounded like a good idea and I settled back on my pillows, picked up *A Prayer for Owen Meany*, and read the first page.

I decided I would be more comfortable if I at least brushed my teeth, and then noticed how dirty the sink was and cleaned it. While going into the kitchen to pour myself a diet RC, I stumbled over about twenty-five hangers and separated them into Bent/Salvageable, Throw Away, and Hang in Closet piles.

I went back to bed, determined to take a Day Off, and tripped over all the overdue library books and magazines and went into my office to make a note to return them to the library. While in there, I found two unanswered letters, a bunch of junk that I stuffed into my working file, then noticed the telephone book on the floor opened to the beauty page and decided to make an appointment to get my hair cut.

Before getting back in bed with my book, I cleaned out my billfold, did a load of wash and the dishes, threw away the "ant hotels" with their No Vacancy signs, sprayed a little Pledge here and there, and then realized the whole house was really dirty and it was Tuesday and I hadn't cleaned on Monday, my usual cleaning day.

I told myself that it didn't matter; that no one cared whether my house was dirty or clean; and that if I wanted to spend a day in bed reading a book, there were no Dirty House Police to arrest me. I read another page, my heart pounding with anxiety. "Something bad will happen if you lay in bed and you aren't sick," some part of me told another part of me.

I made the bed and cleaned the house.

I have written and read a lot about Writer's Block, but I realized there is an even more sinister problem out there that needs to be dealt with: Reader's Block.

For me, there seems to be something hedonistically sinful about reading in the daytime. When the sun goes down and the dishes are done, I climb into bed with a book and feel there is no better way to end a day. But reading—especially a work of fiction—cannot start a day, at least not mine. And yet, if there could be such a thing as a reading instructor and I was one, I would make my students spend at least a semester doing nothing but reading.

I think this reading guilt stems from my childhood, as does everything I can't figure out. My dad—a good, hardworking, industrious grocery store owner with his Protestant Work Ethic flying from his white apron like a flag—once said, with pride in his voice, that he had only read *Black Beauty*. If he found me reading a book in the grass when I was a kid, he would make me mow it, saying something about idle hands and devil's workshops.

(But, once, when my sister and I both had the measles and had to stay in a room with the venetian blinds shut because otherwise we would go blind, he read *Pollyanna* to us with a flashlight. It is still one of those moments that I pull out of my memory bag whenever I feel afraid of the dark.)

When I was growing up, one of my neighbors was Iris. She wore huge turquoise earrings and bracelets, had several dogs and Siamese cats, smoked cigarettes, and had one of the dirtiest houses I'd ever been in. It was my favorite place, and it wasn't just because she had a cute son. Often, when I'd go over to her house, she would be reading a book while listening to Dixieland jazz. Dishes would be piled up from several meals (and she had six kids!), the floor would be sticky, and dustballs and cat hairs were taking up permanent residence under the unmade beds. But she would be reading.

We had continued our friendship until May 21 when she died of cancer of the liver and/or a heart attack. She left her kids a letter. In it she said that she may have not have had the cleanest house in the world but she had always felt that giving the world interesting kids was more important than giving the world a clean house.

Today, while I cleaned, as sort of a tribute to Iris, I didn't turn on the light like my mother always told me to do while running the sweeper. Tomorrow, I'll stay in bed and read a book.

Well, maybe a magazine article.

EVEN COWGIRLS GET THE BLUES
SKIP WILLIAMSON

I Love You, Tom Robbins

The kids and I were lying around watching "Another World" while waiting for "Guiding Light." It was New Year's Eve day. ("Guiding Light" was later pre-empted for yet another football game and the guy who made that decision should have asafetida bags stuffed up his nose holes. Jimmy Carter used to interrupt soaps and look what happened to him.)

Anyway, "Aunt Liz" announced that she was going home to "take a hot bath and read a good book." Everyone else was frantically ringing in the New Year either by kissing or crying or being alone or being together or fainting.

"Oh, doesn't that sound good?" I asked my kids who looked at me like they do when I say I'm not too crazy about

Cyndi Lauper's hair and they feel really sorry for me.

Some time ago, I wrote an article about "How to Tell When You're Middle-aged" and said it was when you couldn't sleep anywhere but in your own bed.

Now, there is another way to tell. If you identify with Aunt Liz more than anyone else on the show and think a hot bath and a good book are a perfect way to spend New Year's Eve, then you're probably middle-aged.

One of the presents my kids always give me for Christmas is some form of bubblebath or pretty soap. This year, they gave me lavender bath baubles that resemble lavender pearls in a lavender dish. I used two in my bath since this time every year I use two of everything: two pieces of candy, two dozen cookies, two pieces of pie, two kinds of cheese dip, and too little will power.

After soaking in the hot tub, I put on my new flannel nightgown and crawled into bed with Tom Robbins' new book *Jitterbug Perfume*, a Christmas gift from my husband. It's the first book I've read in a long, long time that I didn't have to hurry through because it's a month overdue.

As much as I love Tom Robbins' books, I don't recommend them to everyone—especially to my mother. But I love knowing things like Robbins tells me. Here's something I probably never would have known if I hadn't read this book: when they dug up Lenin's body ten years after he died to bury it somewhere else, they found four maraschino cherries in his stomach totally intact. He says, "It is rumored that maraschino cherries are prepared with a chemical resembling formaldehyde, thus can neither be assimilated nor eliminated."

I don't know if that's true or not, but I think it's interesting. I also like people who write sentences like this one: "And the sun pulled a cloud down over its ears." Or this one: "Like jugged bees, the funeral oration droned on." And who can resist a writer who reduces the Middle Ages to these three sentences: "The Middle Ages hangs over history's belt like a beer belly. It is too late now for aerobic dancing or cottage cheese lunches to reduce the Middle

Ages. History will have to wear size-48 shorts forever."

I also think anyone who can write book titles like *Even Cowgirls Get the Blues* is a genius.

As you can tell, I am a fan of Tom Robbins and have been for many years. I even invited him to come live with us several years ago. *Esquire* magazine had asked him to write the column, "Why I Live Where I Live," and he wasn't very nice about telling why he lives where he lives: La Conner, Washington.

After reading the article, I was convinced that he would be tarred and feathered or at least snubbed in the grocery store—so I wrote him a letter asking him if he needed a place to hide out while he wrote his next novel. I invited him to come stay in one of our log cabins at the church camp and I promised not to tell anyone he was here while he was here.

I sent along a picture of our family so he wouldn't think it was a "come-on" and reject me. I noticed my legs were awfully fat, so I took a magic marker and began to do a little creative shading. It wasn't long until I whittled my legs down to broomstick size, but sent it anyway, hoping he would just notice my great tan and not wonder what such a robust body was doing perched on such tiny, tiny legs. I sent the letter via certified mail and still have the receipt he signed.

I also still have the postcard he sent me that was entitled "My Sad Story by Tom Robbins" and showed a "before" and "after" picture of a cartoonish Mr. Robbins. "Before" he was an average-looking American, and "after" ingesting too many hallucinogenic mushrooms, he resembled some sort of wizard. On the flipside of the card were the words: "I have caught my head in a mangle and will be indisposed for Eternity. Despite my condition, however, I am seriously delighted that you braved time, space and Fate itself, in order to communicate with me." (Aw, Tom, it wasn't that hard.)

And then he wrote, in longhand, "Maybe some day I'll take you up on it. Right now, I'm on the road. LOVE, Tom Robbins."

I wrote him another letter, and according to this latest book, he still remembers me.

He dedicated his book to "Donna and the Ohana" and me. Well, I'm not actually mentioned by name, but he did say, "And for those whose letters I still haven't answered."

I think he's crazy about me.

Maybe it was the skinny, middle-aged legs.

Postscript: Tom's next book was entitled *Skinny Legs & All*. Well, well—as they say.

GUN
&
ROSE
SKIP
WILLIAMSON

I'm OK—You've Got Lipstick on Your Teeth

Several years ago I wrote an article entitled "I'm OK—You've Got Lipstick on Your Teeth." It dealt with the fact that even when you think you are OK, there is always a teenager around to tell you that you have lipstick on your teeth or that the color is gross.

This essay was based on the book *I'm O.K., You're O.K.* by Dr. Thomas A. Harris, which was written in 1967. Dr. Harris' theory works for as long as you are reading the book. After that, it becomes silly. No one is totally OK.

When I was a young mother and spent my time hanging around the baby pool, there was another younger mother who also spent her afternoons dipping her perfectly manicured toes into the chlorinated and urine-filled pool. She had perfectly frosted blond hair and perfect fingernails and perfect teeth and a perfect smile. Her eyes were also perfect as well as her tan. Her leopard bikini would have fit a Barbi doll, perfectly.

One day, she leaned over and said, "I hope it don't rain."

I replied, "I hope it *doesn't* either."

After that, I quit hating her. I realized she wasn't perfect—that she would probably have had to write "I will say 'It doesn't,' not 'It don't'" on the blackboard five hundred times if our teacher had still been alive.

There is nothing more pleasant than a flaw. Perhaps that is why the Navajo Indians always put at least one flaw into a rug they were weaving. It was their way of showing the gods they weren't perfect. It's called "The Navajo Rug Theory" and is one that makes sense.

I know that women's lib was supposed to free us from such pettiness. We were supposed to be able to walk into a room full of female strangers and not be jealous and see each other as allies. I don't think it works. I still wish the perfect one wasn't there. "She's snotty," I tell myself, while sneaking glances at her anorexied, tanorexied body.

If we had Dr. Harris' book under our arm and had just been reading page 50 which says, "I'm O.K.—You're O.K., because it is a conscious and verbal decision, [and] can include not only an infinitely greater amount of information about the individual and others, but also the incorporation of not-yet-experienced possibilities which exist in the abstractions of philosophy and religion"—well, maybe we could deal with her. But that's a lot to remember and to think about, and your "adult" tape has to be running.

I think it would be simpler if really perfect-looking people would wear name tags that said: "HI. MY NAME IS RAQUEL. I MAY LOOK PERFECT BUT I CAN'T SPELL VERY WELL."

Or: "HELLO. MY NAME IS CHER AND I REALIZE I HAVE NICE HAIR, BUT YOU SHOULD SEE THE BED WHERE I THREW ALL THE CLOTHES WHEN I COULDN'T FIND ANYTHING TO WEAR."

(Well, maybe they would be more like big sheets of paper instead of name tags, but you get my drift.)

I think we'd all be better off if we started each new day with the premise that "I'm not O.K.—You're not O.K. So what can we do to help each other get through the day?"